PERSECUTION OF THE JEWS

IN RUSSIA

1881.

Reprinted from the "Times," with Map and Appendix.

Printed by
SPOTTISWOODE & CO., NEW-STREET SQUARE, LONDON.
1882.

In the interest of creating a more extensive selection of rare historical book reprints, we have chosen to reproduce this title even though it may possibly have occasional imperfections such as missing and blurred pages, missing text, poor pictures, markings, dark backgrounds and other reproduction issues beyond our control. Because this work is culturally important, we have made it available as a part of our commitment to protecting, preserving and promoting the world's literature. Thank you for your understanding.

MAP OF LOCALITIES IN RUSSIA, MENTIONED IN THIS PAMPHLET.

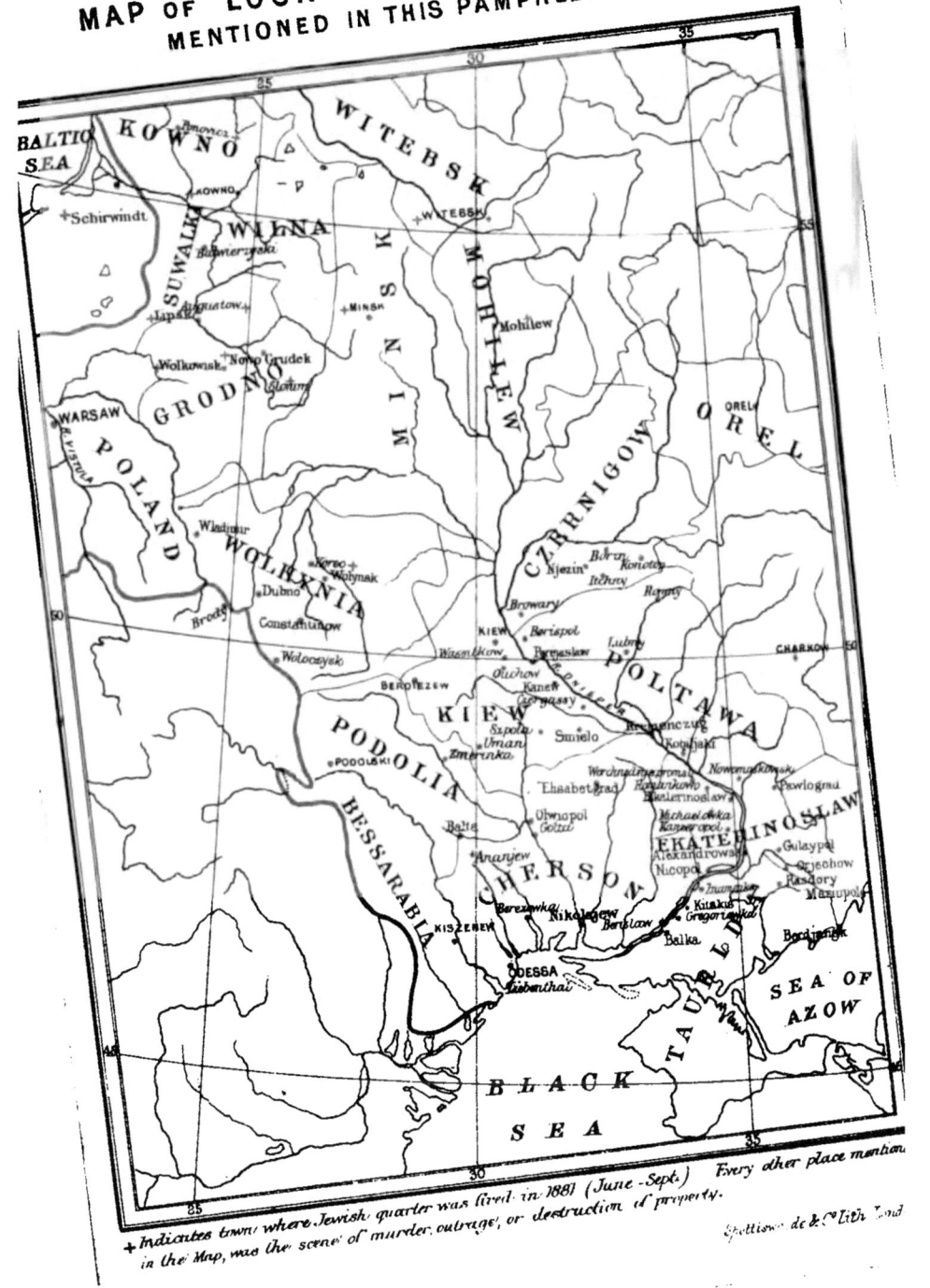

+ Indicates town where Jewish quarter was fired in 1881 (June-Sept.) Every other place mentioned in the Map, was the scene of murder, outrage, or destruction of property.

THE PERSECUTION OF THE JEWS IN RUSSIA.

It is time that the English public should become aware of the character and extent of the persecutions which the Jews of Russia have undergone during the past year. The Warsaw riots have come merely as the last term (as yet) of a series of similar outbreaks which have ravaged the South and West of Russia to an extent of which people outside that country have not the faintest conception. The news which have crossed the borders have been of the most meagre description, chiefly in the form of telegrams announcing that anti-Jewish riots had occurred in such and such a place. Coming at various intervals, they have altogether failed to strike the imagination, and it is due solely to this cause that the public opinion of England, so ready to undertake the cause of suffering humanity, has not given vigorous expression to its feelings of abhorrence. During the past eight months a tract of country, equal in area to the British Isles and France combined, stretching from the Baltic to the Black Sea, has been the scene of horrors that have hitherto only been perpetrated during times of war. Men ruthlessly murdered, tender infants dashed to death, or roasted alive in their own homes, married women the prey of a brutal lust that has often caused their death, and young girls violated in the sight of their relatives by soldiers who should have been the guardians of their honour—these have been the deeds with which the population of Southern Russia has been stained since last April. In the face of these horrors, loss of property is of little moment, yet they have been accompanied by the razing of whole streets inhabited by Jews, by the systematic firing of the Jewish quarters of towns in Western Russia, and by the pillage of all the property on which thousands of Jewish families were dependent for existence.

In addition to all this, many Russian towns have heartlessly seized the occasion to expel from their limits crowds of Jews who have been left by this inhuman and deliberate measure homeless amidst masses infuriated against them. And during these scenes of carnage and pillage the local authorities have stood by with folded arms, doing little or nothing to prevent their occurrence and recurrence, and allowing the ignorant peasantry to remain up to this day under the impression that a ukase existed ordering the property of the Jews to be handed over to their fellow-Russians. So far from publicly expressing reprobation of these outrages, the Minister has issued an edict clearly betraying that the Russian authorities fully share the prejudice of the mob, and contemplate adding to the burdens and inequalities which have been the direct cause of the embittered feeling that has led to these disorders.

Ever since the German anti-Semites had raised an outcry against their Jewish fellow-citizens, it had been feared that the movement would spread to Russia, and there take a form more adapted to the less civilised state of the country. When, therefore, the assassination of the Czar on March 3rd of last year had roused all Russia to the highest pitch of excitement, it was confidently predicted that the approaching Easter would see an outbreak against the Jews. It was said afterwards that the prediction was aided in its fulfilment by Panslavist emissaries from Moscow, who planned all the subsequent troubles. It is at least certain that rumours of a rising had reached Elizabethgrad, and caused the heads of the Jewish community, who form a third of its thirty thousand inhabitants, to apply for special protection from the Governor. No notice was taken of the appeal, and on Wednesday, April 27, the dreaded outbreak took place. A religious dispute in a cabaret led to a scuffle which grew into a general mêlée till the mob obtained possession of the dram-shop and rifled it of its contents. Inflamed by the drink thus obtained, the rioters proceeded to the Jewish quarter, and commenced a systematic destruction of the Jewish shops and warehouses. At first some attempt was made by the Jews to protect their property; but this only served to increase the violence of the mob, which proceeded to attack the dwellings of the Jews and to wreck the synagogues. Amid the horrors that ensued a Jew named Zolotwenski lost his life, and no fewer than thirty Jewesses were outraged. At one place, two young girls, in dread of violation, threw themselves from the windows. Meanwhile the military had been called out, but only to act at first as spectators and afterwards as active participators. One section of the mob formed of rioters and soldiers broke into the dwelling of an old man named Pelikoff, and on his attempting to save his daughter from a fate worse than death, they threw him down from the roof, while twenty soldiers proceeded to work their will on his unfortunate daughter. When seen by the correspondent who narrates this fact, Pelikoff was in a state of hopeless madness, and his daughter completely ruined in mind and body. The whole Jewish quarter was at the mercy of the mob till April the 29th. During the two days of the riots, 500 houses and 100 shops were destroyed, whole streets being razed to the ground. It may be added that the property destroyed and stolen was reckoned at two million roubles.

The evidence of pent-up anti-Jewish passion displayed by these scenes encouraged the foes of the Jews to wider and more systematic attacks. In the excesses that followed, the masses soon got to recognise professional ringleaders from Great Russia. These distributed placards, found afterwards to have been issued from a secret printing-press at Kiew, in which it was declared that the Czar had given his orthodox subjects the property held by the Jews. In most cases the very day on which a riot might be expected was announced beforehand, Sunday and Saints' days being chosen as the days when the lower orders were at liberty. After a week's pause, a whole series of riots broke out, commencing on May 7th at Smielo, near Czergassy, where 13 men were killed and 20 wounded, and 1,600 were left without homes. Next day, Sunday, May 8th, a most serious riot broke out at Kiew, once the capital of Russia, and still an important town, containing 20,000 Jews in a population of 140,000. Here the riot had been definitely announced for the Sunday, and the Jews sent a deputation to the Governor, requesting him to call out his soldiers to prevent disturbance. He bluntly refused, saying that he would not "trouble his soldiers for the sake of a pack of Jews." During the riot which broke out on the day fixed, the police and the soldiers again acted the same part that they had done at Elizabethgrad. The first procedure of the mob had been to storm the dram-shops, and, staving in the brandy casks, to wallow in the spirit. During the period of licence that followed, four Jews were killed, 25 women and girls were violated, of whom five died in consequence, as was proved at the subsequent trials. At the house of Mordecai Wienarski, the mob, disappointed in the search for plunder, caught up his little child three years old and brutally threw it out of the window. The child fell dead at the feet of a company of Cossacks who were drawn up outside, yet no attempt was made to arrest the murderers. At last, when several houses were set on fire, the military received orders to make arrests, which they proceeded to execute with much vigour, making 1,500 prisoners, among whom 150 were Jews arrested for protecting their lives and properties. No less than 2,000 Jews were left without shelter by the dismantling or the burning of their houses, and for the relief of immediate necessities a Kiew Committee soon afterwards had to disburse the sum of £30,000.

Next day similar scenes of violence occurred at Browary, in the neighbourhood of Kiew, in the province of Czernigow. On the same day still more disgraceful deeds were enacted at Berezowka, in the province of Cherson. Here lust seemed more a principal motive than plunder. While the Jews of the village were at synagogue a mob attacked the Jewesses and violated many of them, causing the death of three; others who escaped the worse evil were driven into the river, and nine ultimately died from the effects of the exposure. When the Jews came to the rescue, two of them were killed and a young lad stoned to death.

The neighbourhood of Kiew was again visited on the next day, May 10th, at Konotop and at Wassilkow. At both places the attacks had been planned; at the former, wooden crosses were placed before the doors of Christians that their houses might be spared, while at the latter the day of riot had been announced, and the report diligently spread about that the Czar had given the property of the Jews away. At Wassilkow and in the neighbourhood eight lives were lost, seven at one fell swoop at the inn kept by a Jew named Rykelmann. He was forced to admit the mob to his wine-cellars, and, during his absence in search of assistance, the drunken rioters cut the throats of his wife and six children.

By this time the chief towns and villages of Southern Russia were ablaze with violence and riot. Throughout the whole of the provinces of Cherson, Taurida, Ekaterinoslav, Poltawa, Kiew, Czernigow, and Podolia the notion had spread fast as wildfire that the Jews and their property had been handed over to the tender mercies of the populace, a notion that seems almost justified in the face of the inertness of the Governor-General in checking the riots at Elizabethgrad and Kiew. At Wasiljew the Mayor even read a copy of the supposed ukase to the citizens, and a riot would have ensued had not the village priest done his duty and declared his belief that no such ukase existed. At Alexandrowsk, on the banks of the Dnieper, the operatives carried out what they thought to be the will of the Czar, on May 13th, rendering 300 out of the 400 Jewish families of the place homeless, and destroying property to the amount of 400,000 roubles. As usual, the riots were previously announced, and the appeal to the Governor to send for additional troops proved fruitless. Even after the riots had commenced, a telegram despatched to the capital town of the province, Ekaterinoslav, was delayed for four hours by the Governor before it was sent off. At Ekaterinoslav itself a projected riot was happily prevented by the issue of a proclamation by the local authorities declaring the Jews to be true subjects of the Czar, and entitled to protection of their property. At Polonnoye, near Kiew, a disaster was averted by the forethought of the Mayor, who changed the market-day to Saturday, and on the peasants complaining, he read them a lesson on the utility of the Jews as middle-men, and induced them to promise not to molest their Jewish fellow-citizens.

From Alexandrowsk the instigators paid a visit to the Jewish agricultural colonies in the province of Ekaterinoslav, which have now been established for more than 40 years. The chief centres, Gulaypole, Orjechow, and Marianpol were visited in turn, and though no violence seems to have been done to the persons of the Jews, their farms were almost entirely destroyed. At Orjechow the instigators who led the mob were dressed as police officers, and produced a document falsely purporting to be the proclamation of the Czar. The farming implements were all destroyed, and 500 cattle and 10,000 sheep driven off. At Kamichewka, the Jews adroitly turned the supposed ukase of the Czar into a safeguard. Hearing that the rioters were advancing to attack, they brought the keys of their houses to their Christian neighbours, saying that if the ukase were true, it would be better that their neighbours should have their property than the rioters, and if the ukase proved to be untrue, of course their good neighbours would return the keys. The Christians of the village accordingly repulsed the rioters, and in a few days the Jews of Kamichewka were again in possession of their own property.

Up to this time, the riots had chiefly arisen among the urban populations, but they now spread into the rural districts and reached every little village where even a single Jew resided. A Jew was murdered at Rasdory, a few miles south-east of

Orjechow, and at Znamenka, near Nikopol, on the Dnieper, a Jewish innkeeper named Resser was murdered and his wife dishonoured, after which both were cast into the river. At Balka, also on the bank of the Dnieper, there was only one Jew, Allowicz by name. A band of ruffians went to his house on May 17, and finding him absent, they violated his wife, and, to conceal the crime, set fire to the house while the poor woman lay helpless in it. All this was witnessed by her little daughter, crouched in a ditch hard by. On the preceding day, another tragedy had occurred at Kitzkis, where the house of one Preskoff was set on fire, and he with two little children left to roast in it, while the wife and mother looked on, vainly appealing for mercy, to the ruffianly perpetrators of the crime. At Gregoriewk, a Jewish innkeeper named Rieffmann was cooped in one of his own barrels, and cast into the Dnieper. Again, at Kanzeropol, a man named Enman was murdered brutally and his wife violated and afterwards killed. Such were the deeds that were done on the banks of the Dnieper, during the month of May.

Meantime, the seaport Odessa had likewise been the scene of an anti-Jewish riot. Originally announced for May 13, it was postponed till the Sunday, May 15, without, however, any precautions being taken by the Governor, who had as usual been duly warned of the impending outbreak. Though only lasting for six hours, the riot resulted in the death of a Jew named Handelmann, and eleven cases of violation are reported, one resulting in death. Here the Jews seemed to have been most energetic in their resistance. Of the 800 arrests made, 150 were Jews, 26 of whom were afterwards charged with carrying revolvers without a permit. The police estimated the damage done at 1,137,831 roubles, while those more immediately concerned raised the sum to three millions. Similar scenes took place on the same day at Wolwezysk, on the borders, where a riot had been announced for the Sunday. A week afterwards, the lower orders of Berdyczew rose against the Jews, and on May 24th, a riotous disturbance occurred at Zmerinka, in Podolia.

Thus, within a month of the first outbreak, almost every town of importance in Southern Russia had seen such horrors as we have described. Apart from the influence of the ringleaders, the rioters had no cause to incite them to rapine except the force of contagion, and the impression that the Czar had really transferred all Jewish property to his orthodox subjects. If once this impression had been officially removed, the epidemic would have been checked. In many cases it was distinctly shown that the peasants liked the Jews, and only pillaged because they thought it had been ordered. At Bougaifka, for example, a few days after the peasants had destroyed the property of the Jews, they became contrite, and gave their Jewish neighbours 800 roubles as some compensation for the damage they themselves had caused. In the face of such a fact, it is tolerably certain that if the supposed proclamation had been energetically and officially denied, the riots might never have reached the extent that they eventually did. The contagion spread as far as Saratow in early June, from thence to Astrakhan, and even reached a town near Somsk, in Siberia, and caused an anti-Jewish riot there. The only bright spot in all this gloom was the condition of Poland, where Jews and Poles have always lived in amity. This continued till General Ignatiew directed the Governor of Poland to appoint commissions of experts to consider how the Jews should be dealt with, to which fact persons on the spot attribute the rise of anti-Jewish feeling that culminated in the Warsaw riots. But outside Poland these outbursts of popular prejudice placed a population of nearly two millions in perpetual dread of their lives and property. At times they dared not remove their clothes night or day, fearing that they might have to flee at any moment. Ever since last April, that feeling of fear and insecurity has ruled the lives of all Russian Jews.

Not a month, scarcely a week, has passed since then without some outbreak or other occurring to confirm these fears and render them the more acute. After the Saratow affair, on June

8th, in which 30 Jews were wounded, there was a comparative lull in the more violent forms of outrage. But early in July the neighbourhood of Kiew and the banks of the Dnieper were once more visited by scenes which recall the horrors of the Middle Ages. On Sunday, the 12th, open rioting took place at Perejaslaw, which was characterised by the fact that the mob were led to the attack by the sons of the merchants of the district. Commercial rivalry adding its sting to religious and social differences, the struggle was here of a more violent nature than usual, and, while 30 of the mob were wounded, no less than 200 of the Jews received serious injuries at the hands of their neighbours, and three died in consequence; 176 houses were destroyed, some by fire. At Borispol, on July 21st, scenes occurred during the riots worthy of the worst days of the Commune. Women, for almost the first time, made their appearance on the scene as assailants, and added to its horrors. During the rioting they encouraged their friends on to the fight, and were seen to assist them to violate the Jewesses of the village by holding down the unfortunate creatures. A curious petition afterwards sent from this neighbourhood, demanding, among other things, that Jewesses should not be allowed to wear silks and satins, may throw some light on the motives of these viragos.

The reader will be by this time satiated with the horrible crimes which have been laid before him. The imagination may now be able to take in the full meaning of the bare statement, so frequent during last year, that anti-Jewish riots had taken place in such-and-such a district of Southern Russia. Suffice it then to add that the month of August saw such riots at Njezin on the 2nd, at Lubny on the 8th, at Borzny on the 18th, and at Itchny on the 28th. If September was comparatively free from disorders, the cessation must be attributed rather to the needs of the harvest than to the quieting of the popular mind. For, early in October, the mob attacked the Jews of Balwierzyski, in the government of Suwalki. October 3rd was the Day of Atonement, the most sacred day of the Hebrew calendar, and the mob took the occasion to destroy the synagogue and wreck the Jewish quarter, where one Jew was killed and twenty wounded. Even as late as November, the myth of the spoliation ukase imposed upon the peasantry. On the 15th of that month, a band of a hundred peasants at Czarwona, near Zitomir, pillaged the property of the Jews under that pretext. Lastly, to show the excitable state of the popular mind, the Sarah Bernhardt riots at Kiew on Nov. 18th, and at Odessa on Nov. 27th, proved that a mere suspicion that the actress was a Jewess was sufficient to arouse once more the fury of the mob, and cause them again to attack the Jewish quarter of those towns.

Finally, this catalogue of horrors must be concluded by a reference to the riots at Warsaw, on Christmas and the following days. The detailed events of those days, when 300 houses and 600 shops were pillaged and devastated, and thousands of victims were rendered homeless and reduced to beggary, are doubtless fresh in every one's memory, but certain facts must be again referred to, owing to their typical character. In the first place, the riot was clearly planned, the alarm of fire being simultaneously raised in at least two churches, and the mob being directed by men who spoke Polish with a Russian accent. The culpable neglect of the military authorities of Warsaw in refusing to make use of the 20,000 men forming its garrison, finds its counterpart in the similar behaviour of the Governors of Kiew, Elizabethgrad, and Odessa earlier in the year. The behaviour of the police, who are described as " only interfering to prevent the Jews from protecting themselves," exactly tallies with their behaviour elsewhere. And, finally, the attempts that were made by telegraph officials and others to prevent the true state of the case from reaching the rest of Europe, may serve to account for the extraordinary fact that the enormities of the past nine months have only found the faintest echo in the press of Europe. Thus, while outrages on women were openly committed, the knowledge of this fact has hitherto been kept from crossing the borders.

The outrages we have recounted above, though, no doubt, the most important, are far from including all the similar events that have occurred during the past year. They have been selected from a list of over 160 towns and villages in which cases of riot, rapine, murder, and spoliation have been known to occur during the last nine months of 1881. Out of these, information was collected from about 45 towns and villages in Southern Russia. In these alone are reported 23 murders of men, women, and children, 17 deaths caused by violation, and no fewer than 225 cases of outrages on Jewesses.

Such have been the horrors that throughout the past year have assailed the Israelites who inhabit Russia. Nor is there any indication that these atrocities will cease during the present year, unless the Russian Government will intervene in the sacred cause of civilisation and humanity.

II.

Besides appealing to the blind passions of the mob, the Jew-haters of Russia have during the past year resorted to more systematic efforts to harass the hapless Israelites. The Russian Moujik has a method almost peculiar to himself of expressing his rage and hatred. Moscow is but the most celebrated instance of periods of Russian history when incendiarism has been the order of the day. Whenever the fever point of excitement is reached, arson is usually the direction in which it overflows. So well is this recognised in Russia that the peasants have a technical name for the deliberate firing of towns: the "red cock" is said to crow. During the past year this method of revenge has been resorted to on a large scale against the Jews of Russia, especially in the West. By the end of June the "red cock" had crowed over fifteen towns in Western Russia, including Mohilew, containing 25,000 inhabitants, and Witebsk, with 23,000, and Slonim, with 20,000, as well as smaller towns like Wolkowysk, Schirwindt, Augustowo, Nowo Grudek, Ponovicz, and Lipsk. Many thousands of Jews were rendered homeless by this means, and on July 3, 6,000 Jews lost their homes by fire at Minsk, 4,800 being deprived of every means of subsistence at the same time. The town of Pinsk, in the same province, suffered a like fate. And shortly afterwards a conflagration took place at Koretz, in Wolhynia, in which 30 lives were lost, and 5,000 souls left without a home. Every week added to the number of fires in towns inhabited by Jews, till by the end of September the list extended to forty-one towns. This probably involved the loss of home to 20,000 Jews.

To the mass of homeless and penniless creatures in Southern Russia must be added the many victims of pillage. The violence of the mobs often wrecked whole streets of houses as completely as any fire, and we know of 2,000 who were thus rendered homeless at Kiew, 1,600 at Smielo, 1,000 at Konotop, 600 at Ouchow, and 300 at Obuchow. The value of property destroyed in the South has been reckoned to reach £16,000,000 sterling.

It is possible that an aggregate of a hundred thousand Jewish families has thus been reduced to poverty. The ranks of the ruined were increased by those who dared not apply for their just debts, while in many cases the peasantry have deliberately "Boycotted" the Jews. It must be further remembered that in several places the Jews anticipated riots by evacuating their homes; thus, near Perejaslaw, after the riot at that place, no fewer than 17 villages in the neighbourhood were deserted by the Jews, and the same doubtless took place in other localities. Men have fled from the villages in which they have resided all their lives. Even after the events of Kiew the Jews of the neighbourhood, fearing the spread of disorder, crowded at the rate of one hundred families a day into the town which had so lately shown itself hostile. Others fled towards the borders, and during the summer months a camp of refugees in the open air, at Podwoloczyska, contained no less than 1,500 souls, including children of the tenderest age. A few, who still possessed some means, attempted to flee across the frontier, but many were stopped. Of 5,000 who managed to reach Brody, on the Austrian border, in a perfectly helpless state, 2,000 still remain there, huddled in cellars. What horrors are in store for the thousands and thousands who have been left to face the rigours of a Russian winter with no resources, no one outside Russia can possibly imagine.

Meanwhile, the municipalities, with the connivance of the local governments, have taken every means in their power to add to the misery of the situation. With rough logic, they argued that, as these riots were directed against the Jews, if there had been no Jews, there would have been no riots. They accordingly petitioned the governors of their provinces to issue orders for the expulsion of the Jews from towns in which they had no legal right of domicile. The Jews of Russia are only allowed to reside in twenty-eight of its provinces, often only in certain towns, and the number of permits to reside is, at least theoretically, limited. For the last twenty years, however, these barbarous laws have been somewhat allowed to fall into desuetude, and many Jews have ventured beyond the narrow limits assigned to them. Leaving aside the general question, it was clearly a most heartless act to add to the miseries of the Jewish population at the moment when the mob were eagerly scanning the disposition of the authorities to discover to what lengths they might proceed with impunity. Whatever be the legality of the measure, the occasion for introducing its rigorous enforcement was inhumanly inopportune, and lays the corporations who enforced it liable to a charge of complicity with the more lawless persecutors of the Jews. At Kiew, for example, even before the excitement had entirely subsided, the Governor ordered a stringent scrutiny of the right of domicile among the Jews of that town. By July 29th the strict enforcement of these harsh regulations had resulted in the expulsion of 4,000 Jews, and quite recently new rules have been issued in Kiew, as well as Odessa, still further limiting the number of Jews capable of residing in either city. At Liebenthal, near Odessa, the municipality, of course with the permission of the Governor of Odessa, expelled from fifteen to twenty Jewish families, and imposed a fine of fifty roubles upon anyone harbouring a Jew for a single night. From Podolsk 100 families have been expelled, while whole regions of Podolia have been relentlessly cleared of the Jews; the towns of Kromonitz, Dubno, Constantinow, Wladimir, and Wolinsk being the principal offenders. More to the east the town of Charkow expelled Jews at the beginning of August. At Orel, in the Government of that name, the expulsion has recently taken place on a large scale, and under peculiarly cruel circumstances. In that town 900 families of Jews, numbering 5,000 souls, have hitherto dwelt in peace and goodwill with their neighbours. Soon after the outbreak of the disturbances the Governor of Orel gave orders that all Jews must quit its bounds by September 1st. When that day arrived a further grace was allowed them till October 25th, and on the latter day the Jewish congregation met for the last time in the synagogue, and after tearful prayers removed the sacred scrolls and left in mournful procession the town that had been their home. Nearly 400 of them, however, did not even possess the means of departure, and ventured to remain, only to be thrust out by the police into the snow on the following night. In other places, where no legal objection could be taken to the domicile of the Jews, petitions were sent by the authorities requesting the imposition of all sorts of restrictions. They desire to restrict Jewish commerce in grain, to limit the sending of Jewish children to the higher gymnasia and universities, thus stultifying their own complaints as to the want of culture among the Jews.

Many of the local Commissions would prevent Jews from holding "harandas," erroneously described as "dram-shops," but really general stores, at which wine and spirits are sold. We have already referred to the Perejaslaw petition, that Jewesses be not allowed to wear silks and satins. These expulsions and petitions have formed the sole answer which the town councils of Russia have given to the Jewish question.

Meanwhile, what has been done in this emergency? It is by no means difficult to suggest what could and should have been done from the first appearance of anti-Jewish feeling in the south. If orders had been given and published that every Governor-General should supply Jewish communities with a guard, on application from the Rabbi and the elders of the community; if an edict had been passed rendering all damage to Jewish property by riots chargeable to the communal rates of the town or village; if, above all, a proclamation had been issued declaring that all Jewish subjects were as much entitled to protection of life and property as their orthodox fellow-citizens, and denying the existence of any ukase purporting to "convey" their property, it is safe to assert that the disorders would not have spread far, and certainly would not have lasted long. Instead of this, at Kiew instructions were issued that the military should not be called out till the last extremity.

As early as May 23rd, the Czar, having been appealed to by a deputation of the Jews of St. Petersburg, headed by Baron Günzburg, expressed his intention of dealing with the evil. Accordingly Count Kutaissow was despatched to the South to make inquiries. He returned, it would seem, with the result that still further inquiries were necessary. General Ignatiew now took the opportunity to introduce a system by which the Zemstvos, or provincial assemblies, might be superseded by local committees of experts on this special subject; and on September 3rd the following rescript was issued.

"For some time the Government has given its attention to "the Jews, and to their relations to the rest of the inhabitants "of the empire, with the view of ascertaining the sad condition "of the Christian inhabitants, brought about by the conduct "of the Jews in business matters.

"For the last twenty years the Government has endea-"voured, in various ways, to bring the Jews near to its other "inhabitants, and has given them almost equal rights with the "indigenous population. The movements, however, against "the Jews, which began last spring in the South of Russia, and

"extended to Central Russia, prove incontestably that all its
"endeavours have been of no avail, and that ill-feeling prevails
"now as much as ever between the Jewish and the Christian
"inhabitants of those parts. Now, the proceedings at the trial
"of those charged with rioting, and other evidence, bear witness
"to the fact that the main cause of those movements and riots
"—to which the Russians, as a nation, are strangers—was but a
"commercial one, and is as follows:

"During the last twenty years the Jews have gradually pos-
"sessed themselves of not only every trade and business in all
"its branches, but also of a great part of the land by buying or
"farming it. With few exceptions they have, as a body, devoted
"their attention, not to enriching or benefiting the country,
"but to defrauding by their wiles its inhabitants, and particu-
"larly its poor inhabitants. This conduct of theirs has called
"forth protests on the part of the people, as manifested in acts
"of violence and robbery. The Government, whilst on the
"one hand doing its best to put down the disturbances, and to
"deliver the Jews from oppression and slaughter, have also on
"the other hand thought it a matter of urgency and justice to
"adopt stringent measures in order to put an end to the
"oppression practised by the Jews on the inhabitants, and to
"free the country from their malpractices, which were, as is
"known, the cause of the agitation.

"With this view, it has appointed Commissions (in all the
"towns inhabited by Jews), whose duty it is to inquire into the
"following matters:

"I. What are the trades of the Jews which are injurious to
"the inhabitants of the place?

"II. What makes it impracticable to put into force the
"former laws limiting the rights of the Jews in the
"matter of buying and farming land, the trade in in-
"toxicants and usury?

"III. How can those laws be altered so that they shall no
"longer be enabled to evade them, or what new laws are
"required to stop their pernicious conduct in business?

"IV. Give (besides the answers to the foregoing questions)
 "the following additional information:
"(a) On the usury practised by the Jews in their dealings
 "with Christians, in cities, towns, and villages.
"(b) The number of public-houses kept by Jews in their
 "own name, or in that of a Christian.
"(c) The number of persons in service with Jews, or under
 "their control.
"(d) The extent (acreage) of the land in their possession,
 "by buying or farming.
"(e) The number of Jewish agriculturists.

"In addition to the above-named information to be supplied, every Commission is empowered to report on such conduct and action of the Jews as may have a local interest and importance, and to submit the same to the Ministry."

That after the events of May, June, and July, any person in authority in Russia should in August have been thinking of aught else but the protection of Jewish lives and the honour of Jewish women is the first surprise that meets us in this remarkable document. But that no word of reprimand should be addressed to those that had indulged in such misdeeds is a severer surprise still; the only allusion to the whole catalogue of horrors being couched in the half-apologetic allusion to "protests" that have taken so deplorable a form. It is certain that the direct cause of the objection of the Russians to their Jewish fellow-citizens is the natural result of the Russian laws which restrict their rights and mark them off from the rest of the nation. It is the lesson taught by all experience, that the only solution of the Jewish question is the granting of full equality. It is absolutely certain that the whole body of Jews, forming one-eighth of the population amid which they dwell, cannot be accused of "exploitation," or "usury," as imputed by the rescript, the fact being that the chief industries of Russia are in the hands of the thrifty and hard-working Jews. Again, objection to innkeeping by Jews is clearly a gross injustice, seeing that statistics show drunkenness to be more prevalent in provinces where Jews do not reside. But, waiving all this, surely the poor women who had been violated, the little children who had been murdered, the farmers who had been robbed of their cattle and implements, could not be accused of these charges, and it was accordingly a refinement of cruelty to issue this document, teeming with animus at a time when the passions of the mob had been raised against all Jews without distinction of person, occupation, age, or sex. The Jewish question at the present moment is not whether the Jews should be prevented from competing with the Russians in certain trades, but whether the lives of three millions and a half of Jews shall be left at the mercy of the passions of the mob. A document like this, far from helping to solve the question, rather adds to its complexity by showing clearly to the populace that the authorities share their prejudices. The appointments to commissions showed the same bias: at the head of the Kiew Commission was placed General Drudkoff, the Governor of Kiew, who initiated the proceedings of the first meeting by declaring "either I or the Jews must go." On another Commission was placed M. Chigaryne, whose only claim to be considered an expert on the Jewish question was that he had written a pamphlet entitled "The Annihilation of the Jews."

At Odessa, the first Commission was dismissed because it had recommended the only true solution of the questions put by the Minister for the Interior, the granting to the Jews full equality of rights and equal liberty of settlement with their fellow-citizens of other creeds. A second Commission was thereupon appointed with views more in consonance with the spirit of the rescript. When the Governor of Warsaw, Count Albidinski, was ordered to publish the circular, he at first refused, saying that Jews and Poles had always lived on such friendly terms that no Commission was necessary. He was, however, forced to publish the rescript, and competent observers attribute the rise of anti-Semitic feeling in Warsaw mainly to this publication.

These acts, and the tone of the circular itself, made clear to the Commissions what was expected of them. They have accordingly made recommendations, which will, if adopted, bring back all the horrors of the Middle Ages on the unfortunate Jews of Russia. Thus, among other proposals, they have advised that Jews should not be allowed to build synagogues or establish schools and orphan asylums, that they should not be permitted to reside in villages, nor own houses or landed property, that Jews should not lease factories or sell spirituous liquors, or be apothecaries. Beside this, it is rumoured that it is intended to restrict still further the right of domicile, and to allow no Jew to reside within eighty miles of the borders. In short, it seems to be the intention to make Russia an impossible home for the Jews, or perhaps even to doom them to complete extinction. The Russo-Jewish question may, therefore, be summed up in these words: Are three and a half millions of human beings to perish because they are Jews?

APPENDIX.

LIST
OF
167 PLACES IN RUSSIA
WHERE JEWS HAVE BEEN
PERSECUTED
IN 1881.

Town	Government	Date	Nature of Persecution
Alexandrowsk	Ekaterinoslav	May 13	Riot by operatives; 400,000 R. lost; announced previously; appeal to Governor in vain; telegram stopped 4 hours; 300 out of 400 families left desolate; woman rendered lunatic.
Ananiew	Cherson	May 9	Riot; all houses of Jews destroyed.
Apouchtipi	Ekaterinoslav	May 15–20	Riot; agricultural colony pillaged.
Astrakhan	Astrakhan	August 30	Arrest made by police of instigators alleging ukase.
Augustowo	Suwalki	June	Fire in Jewish quarter.
Balanouska	Podolia	June	Riot; pillage.
Balka	Taurida	May 17	Wife of innkeeper Allowicz outraged, then roasted in the house set fire to, in presence of daughter.
Balta	Podolia	July	Threats sent to Jews to fire it.
Balwierzyski	Suwalki	October 3 (*Yom Kippur*)	Riot; 1 Jew killed, 20 severely wounded; synagogue destroyed.
Bereznom	Czernigow	about May 28	Riot.
Berezowka	Cherson	May 21	Riot; over 100 Jewesses violated, several forced into river; 9 died from exposure, 3 from violation; 2 men killed; boy stoned to death on Sunday May 22nd.
Berislaw	Cherson	May	One Jew killed and house burned down; another roasted alive in own house; outrages.
Berizan	Kiew	July 21	Riot; houses destroyed
Bierdjansk	Taurida	July 1	Municipal Council petitioned for expulsion.
Blagourechtensk	Ekaterinoslav	about May 15–20	Riot; pillage of agricultural colony.
Bongaifka	Kiew	May–June	After riot peasants offered 800 r. compensation.
Bobryki	Poltawa	May 19	Riot; pillage; houses destroyed.
Borispol	Kiew	July 21–24	Riot; Jewish quarter burnt down; women help to pillage, and brought out their children to witness the scene; women held down Jewesses to be violated; 30 houses destroyed.

25

Borzny	Czernigow	August 18-19	Riot; pillage; houses destroyed.
Browary	Czernigow	May 9	Destroyed property, but no personal injury.
Charkow	Charkow	August	Jews expelled.
Chvodom	...	June	Jewish quarter fired.
Constantino	Wolhynia	November	Jews expelled.
Czarekonstantinofka	Ekaterinoslav	May 15-20	Riot; pillage of agricultural colony.
Czarwona	Wolhynia, near Zitomir	November 15	100 rioters attacked Jews, alleging ukase.
Czerbaka	Taurida	May 20-28	Riot; pillage; houses destroyed.
Czergassy	Melitopol, C. Wasiljew Kiew	May–July	Riot.
Czernigow	Czernigow	About June 1	Mob raised by soldier Korotych, but riot prevented by mayor.
Czumaki	Ekaterinoslav	May–July	Riot.
Czykaki	Poltawa	About June 1	Riot.
Dubno	Wolhynia	November	Jews expelled.
Dzemailowtse	Czernigow, near Njezin	About August 27	Riot; 8 arrested.
Dziewica	Czernigow, near Njezin	About August 30	Riot; an elder and a journalist molested for interfering in favour of Jews.
Ekaterinoslav	Ekaterinoslav	May 18-20	Riot; prevented by announcement that Jews are Russian subjects.
Elizabethgrad	Cherson	April 27	Riots; riots were announced and planned; origin in "blood accusation"; merchandise thrown in street; Cossacks present; one Jew killed, name Zolotwenski; two young girls threw themselves from second story; 500 houses and 100 shops destroyed; military would not interfere; 30 cases of violation. Protecting his daughter, an old man, Pelikoff, thrown from roof and rendered insane; 3 persons killed in the districts. Soldiers shared in plunder.
Frederikowka	Wolhynia, near Woloczysk	May 15	Riot; pillage.
Gadacza	Czernigow	May	Riot.
Garadisch	...	June	Jewish quarter burnt.
Gaygoula	Ekaterinoslav	May 20	Riot; pillage; agricultural colony.
Golta	Cherson, near Olwiopol	May 7	Riot; more than 50 arrested; riot foretold.

Town	Government.	Date	Nature of Persecution
Gorkaya	Ekaterinoslav	About May 20	Riot; pillage of agricultural colony.
Grafski	Ekaterinoslav	May 17	Riot; pillage; alleged ukase appealed to.
Gregoriewk	Taurida	About May 20	Riot; innkeeper Kieffmann placed in one of his own barrels and cast into Dnieper.
Gulaypole	Ekaterinoslav	May 17	Riot stopped by appeal to elders; agricultural community.
Gusarka	Ekaterinoslav	May 15–20	Riot; pillage of agricultural colony.
Hausarki	Ekaterinoslav	May 15–20	Riot; pillage of agricultural colony.
Hermanowka	Kiew	About June 5	Riot.
Ianchikraka	Taurida	About May 20	Riot; all Jewish houses destroyed.
Itchny	Czernigow	Sunday, Aug. 28	Riot; further riot, releasing rioters previously arrested.
Jagary	Near Benen	August 23	Jewish quarters fired; 213 houses destroyed.
Jereminka	Cherson	May 10	Riot; houses destroyed.
Kainsk	Tomsk (Siberia)	June	Riot.
Kalaslina	Ekaterinoslav, border of Poltawa	May	Riot; houses dismantled.
Kamychewary	Ekaterinoslav	About May 20	Riot prevented by market changed to Saturday.
Kazieneo	Poland	June 15	Jews prevented riot by handing over property on account of supposititious ukase.
Kamishowaka	Ekaterinoslav	May	Riot; pillage.
Kamychewka	Ekaterinoslav	May 15	Riot.
Kanew	Kiew	May	Riot; Jew, Enman, killed; wife violated and killed.
Kanzeropol	Ekaterinoslav	About May 20	Riot; previously announced: Governor refused to interfere "for a pack of Jews"; 4 Jews killed; 25 women violated; 5 Jewesses died from outrage; child (3 years old) of Mordecai Wienanki killed by being thrown out of window; 150 Jews arrested; 2,000 Jews left homeless; 3,000,000 roubles lost.
Kiew	Kiew	Sunday, May 8	
		June	Stricter laws of domicile applied; 4,000 (out of 20,000) Jews expelled.
		November 18	Sarah Bernhardt riots.

Kiszenew		Bessarabia	May 14	Riot.
Kitzkis		Taurida	May 16	Riot; Preskoff and 2 little children burnt in own house in presence of his wife; 25 houses burnt to ground.
Kobeljaki		Poltawa	About May 20	Chief Rabbi severely wounded.
Konotop		Czernigow	May 10	Riot; Wooden crosses placed before Christian doors to distinguish them.
Konski		Ekaterinoslav	May 15–20	Riot; pillage, agricultural colony.
Kopoczar		Kiew	About June 5	Riot; pillage; 9 families ruined.
Kopalchuka		Wolhynia, border Galicia	About Sept. 20	Riot; pillage.
Kopanie		Ekaterinoslav, near Orjechow	About May 20	Riot; houses destroyed.
Koretz		Wolhynia	July 5	Fire; 5,000 souls homeless, 39 burned; 1,010 houses destroyed.
Korsoon		Kiew	April 28	Riot.
Kowno		Kowno	July	Fire.
Krasnosulka		Ekaterinoslav	May 20	Attempted riot.
Kratanowo		...	June	Fire.
Kremenczug		Poltawa	May	Riot; 2 Jews killed.
Krinko		Ekaterinoslav, near Poltawa	May	Riot.
Kremye Kotchin		Czernigow	August	Riot; Jews afterwards "Boycotted."
Kromonitz		Podolia	November	Jews expelled.
Liebenthal		Cherson	August 6	20 Jewish families expelled; fine of 50 roubles put on harbouring a Jew.
Liliaki		Poltawa	July 20	Riot; all Jewish shops destroyed.
Lipsk		Suwalki	June	Jewish quarter fired.
Lorew		Minsk	May 20	Attempted riot by suppositious ukase.
Lonborzy		Poltawa	July 28	Riot; Jewish houses destroyed.
Lozowy		Ekaterinoslav	May 13	Riot; pillage of agricultural colony.
Lubny		Poltawa	August 8	Riot; houses destroyed; one person killed.
Ludwinow		Kiew	May 10	Riot; spoliation, ukase referred to.
Mala Tokinaliki		Ekaterinoslav, near Orjechow	About May 20	Riot; houses destroyed.
Maskowtzkye		Poltawa	June	Riot.

Town	Government	Date	Nature of Persecution
Megeretz	Ekaterinoslav	May 15-20	Riot; pillage of agricultural colony.
Menie	Czernigow	About May 20	Riot; 16 shops sacked.
Michaelowka	Ekaterinoslav	May	Riot; Jew killed; Jewish innkeeper and family burnt alive.
Minsk	Minsk	July 3	Fire; 6,000 homeless.
Mohilew	Mohilew	June	Fire.
Najednaja	Ekaterinoslav	May 20	Riot; agricultural colony.
Nichaefka	Ekaterinoslav	May 18	Riot; agricultural colony; Jews expelled without notice.
Nicholaiew	Cherson	May 15	Riot.
Nikopol	Ekaterinoslav	May	Riot; pillage
Njezin [Nigyne]	Czernigow	August 2	Riot; pillage; houses destroyed.
Noguenie	Podolia	June 9	Riot; pillage.
Nowoczerkask	...	September 1	Jews expelled.
Nowogeorgruwsk	Kiew	May	Riot.
Nowogradek	Grodno	June	Fire.
Nowomoskowsk	Poltawa	May	Riot.
Nowopaulowka	Ekaterinoslav	About May 20	Riot; houses destroyed.
Nowosulki	Ekaterinoslav	May 17	Riot.
Obuchow	Kiew	About May 28	Riot; 300 families homeless.
Odessa	Cherson	May 15	Riot; announced for May 13; Governor appealed to in vain; Jew Handelmann killed; 11 Jewesses violated, one of whom died; loss of property, 1,137,800 roubles. Stricter laws of domicile.
Olchana	Kiew	June	Sarah Bernhardt riots.
Olwiopol	Cherson	November 27	Riot; spoliation ukase referred to.
Orjechow	Ekaterinoslav	May 9	Riot.
		May 7	Ringleaders dressed as police officers bearing supposed ukase; agricultural colony, 500 cattle, 10,000 sheep driven off.

Orel	Orel	October 25	Jews expelled to the number of 5,000; 400 Jews thrust out into snow on night of October 26.
Ouchow	Kiew	May	Riot; 240 Jewish families homeless.
Pawlezrad	Ekaterinoslav	May	Riot.
Peregonow	Kiew	May 9	Riot; spoliation ukase referred to.
Perejaslaw	Poltawa	July 12	Riot, previously announced, headed by local tradesmen; fire, 176 houses destroyed; 17 villages in neighbourhood deserted; 3 killed.
Pinsk	Minsk	August	Petition for anti-Jewish restrictions.
Petrowki	Ekaterinoslav	May	Jewish quarter fired.
Podolsk	Podolia	May 20	Riot; Jewish family murdered.
		July	100 Jewish families expelled.
Podstepni	Taurida	May 15–20	Riot.
Podwoloczyska	Podolia	June	1,500 Jews driven from their homes.
		Nov. 10	Sarah Bernhardt riot.
Pokrowsk	Ekaterinoslav	May 15	Riot; imminent, but prevented.
Polonnoye	Kiew	May 22	Riot prevented by postponement of market to Saturday.
Polselvi		June	Fire in Jewish quarter.
Poltawa	Poltawa	May	Riot.
Ponovicz	Kowno	June	Jewish quarter fired.
Potsk	Kiew	May 15	Riot.
Preobajensk	Ekaterinoslav	May 17	Riot; houses dismantled.
Prochorowka	Kiew	May	Riot.
Radsk		June	Jewish quarter fired.
Rasdory	Ekaterinoslav	May	Riot; one Jew murdered; all Jews driven forth.
Rowno .	Poltawa	About June 9	Riot; pillage; Jewess killed.
Romanowka	Ekaterinoslav	May	Riot; 3 Jewesses violated.
Rzanie	Ekaterinoslav	About July 10	Riot; rioters released.
Saratow	Saratow	June 8	Riot; 30 Jews wounded.
Schirwindt	Suwalki	June	Fire in Jewish quarter.
Seminowka	Poltawa	About July 20	Riot; pillage.
Senelmkowo	Ekaterinoslav	June	Riot.

Town	Government	Date	Nature of Persecution
Setel	...	June	Jewish quarter fired.
Skopetz	Poltawa	May	Riot.
Skopzy	Poltawa	July 28	Riot; Jewish houses destroyed.
Sladkonodnaya	Ekaterinoslav	May 20	Riot.
Slonim	Grodno	June	Fire in Jewish quarter.
Smila	Kiew	May 15	Riot; 13 Jews killed, 20 wounded; 1,600 rendered homeless.
Swobodka	Kiew	About May 20	Riot.
Szpola	Kiew	May 9	Riot.
Tarnoruda	Podolia	May 15	Riot; pillage.
Terpienje	Taurida	May 20	Riot; child of Jew Skotloff murdered.
Toskopzy	Poltawa	July 28	Riot; Jewish houses destroyed.
Trondoubolowke	Ekaterinoslav	About May 20	Riot; pillage of agricultural colony.
Uman	Kiew	May 9	Riot.
Warsaw	Poland	December 25	Riot: planned; alarm raised in four churches simultaneously, military not called out; 12 Jews killed, 6,000 homeless; 2,000,000 roubles destroyed; outrages. Lasted three days.
Wasansk	Ekaterinoslav	June	Riot prevented by altering market to Saturday.
Wasiljew	Taurida	May	Mayor read the confiscation ukase.
Wasilkow	Kiew	May 10	Riot announced; the spoliation ukase referred to; one Jew killed in neighbourhood; wife and 6 children of innkeeper Bykelmann murdered.
Waylowtzye	Poltawa	June	Riot.
Werchednjepromst	Ekaterinoslav	May	Riot; 5 Jews killed.
Wiktorowka	Cherson	May 10	Riot.
Witebsk	Witebsk	June	Fire in Jewish quarter.
Wladimir	Wolhynia	October	Jews expelled.
Wojtowzy	Poltawa	July 28	Riot; Jewish houses destroyed.
Wolatcaisk	Wolhynia	May 14	Riot.
Wolinsk	Wolhynia	October	Jews expelled.

Wolkowisk	Grodno	June	Fire.
Wolwczysk	Podolia	May 15	Riot; announced; 30 houses destroyed.
Woskresienka	Ekaterinoslav	May 17	Riot; Jewish houses destroyed; agricultural colony.
Zmerinka	Podolia	May 24	Riot; houses destroyed.
Znamenka	Taurida	May 17	Jew, Resser, killed, his wife outraged, and both thrown into Dnieper.
Znki	Poltawa	June	Riot.

LONDON: PRINTED BY
SPOTTISWOODE AND CO., NEW-STREET SQUARE
AND PARLIAMENT STREET

Printed by Libri Plureos GmbH in Hamburg, Germany